SDiabetic
Soup

Side Salads
Apple-Walnut Salad with Blue Cheese-Honey Vinaigrette 4
Roasted Vegetable Salad. 6
Cranberry-Apple Gelatin Salad 8
Marinated Tomato Salad. .10
Italian Crouton Salad 12
Raspberry Mango Salad 14
Greens and Broccoli Salad with Peppy Vinaigrette. 16
Lime-Ginger Cole Slaw 18
Fresh Cranberry-Pineapple Salad 20
Greens and Pears with Maple-Mustard Dressing 22

Main-Course Salads
Mediterranean Chicken Salad 24
Finger-Lickin' Chicken Salad 26
Turkey Club Salad 28
Chicken and Apple Spring Green Salad with Poppy Seed Dressing 30
Gazpacho Shrimp Salad 32
Healthy Chopped Salad 34
Zesty Taco Salad. 36
Three-Pepper Tuna Salad .38
Chicken and Pasta Salad with Kalamata Olives. 40
Salmon and Green Bean Salad with Pasta 42

Super Soups
Winter Squash Soup 44
Country Sausage and Bean Soup 46
Deep Bayou Chowder. 48
Beef and Veggie Soup 50
Chilled Roasted Red Pepper Soup. 52
Hearty Lentil and Root Vegetable Soup 54
French Peasant Soup 56
Main-Dish Chicken Soup .58
Cuban-Style Black Bean Soup. 60
Creamy Cauliflower Bisque 62
Tomato-Herb Soup 64

Soups and Salads

Maintaining a healthy diet is important for everyone. But, for people with diabetes it is more than important—it is vital to managing blood sugars. The recipes in this book were selected specifically for people with diabetes in mind, but they are also healthy for the entire family.

page 20   page 40   page 62

Soups and salads can help with weight management

Eating foods such as soups and salads can be very beneficial. When made using nutritious low-fat ingredients, they make you feel full quicker and longer so you are less tempted to overeat or snack on higher calorie foods. They are also usually lower in calories which helps with weight management. And, most salads are made with raw vegetables which are proven to have more nutritional value than cooked vegetables.

One word of caution: When eating a salad, be very careful to select a low-fat or low-calorie dressing. Some salad dressings are very high in fat and carbohydrates, so choose your dressing wisely.

Facts About the Recipes

All the recipes in this book are based on the principles of sound nutrition, making them perfect for the entire family. These recipes are not to be used as a substitute for medically approved meal plans.

The Dietary Exchanges are based on the Exchange Lists for Meal Planning developed by the American Diabetes Association and The American Diabetic Association. Every effort has been made to check the accuracy of these numbers. However, because numerous variables account for a wide range of values in certain foods, all analyses that appear in the book should be considered approximate.

- The analysis of each recipe includes all the ingredients that are listed in that recipe, except for ingredients labeled as "optional" or "for garnish." Nutritional analysis is provided for the primary recipe only, not for the recipe variations.

- If a range is offered for an ingredient, the first amount given was used to calculate the nutritional information.

- If an ingredient is presented with an option ("3 tablespoons margarine or butter," for example), the *first* item listed was used to calculate the nutritional information.

Side Salads

Apple-Walnut Salad with Blue Cheese-Honey Vinaigrette

- ¼ cup chopped walnuts
- 1 tablespoon white wine vinegar
- 2 teaspoons olive oil
- 2 teaspoons honey
- ¼ teaspoon salt
- ⅛ teaspoon black pepper
- 2 tablespoons crumbled blue cheese
- 1 large head Bibb lettuce, separated into leaves
- 1 small Red Delicious apple, thinly sliced
- 1 small Granny Smith apple, thinly sliced

1. Place walnuts in small skillet over medium heat. Cook and stir 5 minutes or until fragrant and lightly toasted. Transfer to plate to cool.

2. Combine vinegar, oil, honey, salt and pepper in small bowl; whisk until smooth. Stir in cheese.

3. Divide lettuce and apples evenly among 4 plates. Drizzle dressing evenly over each salad; top with walnuts. *Makes 4 servings*

<u>**Nutrients per serving:**</u> ¼ of total recipe

Calories	133	Carbohydrate	20 g
Calories from Fat	37 %	Cholesterol	3 mg
Fat	6 g	Sodium	135 mg
Saturated Fat	1 g	Fiber	2 g
Protein	4 g		

Dietary Exchanges: 1 Vegetable, 1 Fruit, 1 Fat

Roasted Vegetable Salad

1 cup sliced mushrooms
1 cup carrot slices
1 cup chopped green or yellow bell pepper
1 cup cherry tomatoes, halved
½ cup chopped onion
2 tablespoons chopped pitted kalamata or black olives
2 teaspoons lemon juice, divided
1 teaspoon dried oregano
1 teaspoon olive oil
½ teaspoon black pepper
3 cups packed torn stemmed spinach or baby spinach

1. Preheat oven to 375°F. Combine mushrooms, carrots, bell pepper, tomatoes, onion, olives, 1 teaspoon lemon juice, oregano, oil and black pepper in large bowl; toss until evenly coated.

2. Spread vegetables in single layer on baking sheet. Bake 20 minutes, stirring once during baking. Stir in remaining 1 teaspoon lemon juice. Serve warm over spinach. *Makes 2 servings*

Nutrients per serving: ½ of total recipe

Calories	121	Carbohydrate	20 g
Calories from Fat	29 %	Cholesterol	0 mg
Fat	4 g	Sodium	314 mg
Saturated Fat	<1 g	Fiber	6 g
Protein	5 g		

Dietary Exchanges: 3 Vegetable, 1 Fat

Cranberry-Apple Gelatin Salad

2 packages (4-serving size each) sugar-free cranberry-flavored or any red-colored gelatin

1½ cups boiling water

2 cups sugar-free lemon-lime-flavored soda

1 cup finely chopped red apple

½ cup finely chopped celery

3 tablespoons finely chopped walnuts

1. Dissolve gelatin in boiling water in medium bowl. Refrigerate 15 minutes. Stir in soda. Cover; chill 1 to 1½ hours or until partially set.

2. Fold in apple, celery and walnuts. Pour into 6-cup gelatin mold or 12 (6-ounce) custard cups. Cover; refrigerate at least 4 hours or until set. If using gelatin mold, remove from mold. *Makes 12 servings*

Nutrients per serving: ½ cup salad

Calories	28	Carbohydrate	3 g
Calories from Fat	43 %	Cholesterol	0 mg
Fat	1 g	Sodium	58 mg
Saturated Fat	<1 g	Fiber	1 g
Protein	1 g		

Dietary Exchanges: Free

Marinated Tomato Salad

1½ cups white wine or tarragon vinegar
½ teaspoon salt
¼ cup finely chopped shallots
2 tablespoons finely chopped chives
2 tablespoons fresh lemon juice
¼ teaspoon white pepper
2 tablespoons extra-virgin olive oil
6 plum tomatoes, quartered
2 large yellow tomatoes,* sliced horizontally
    into ½-inch thick slices
16 red cherry tomatoes, halved
16 small yellow pear tomatoes,* halved (optional)
    Sunflower sprouts (optional)

Substitute 10 plum tomatoes, quartered, for yellow tomatoes and yellow pear tomatoes, if desired.

1. Combine vinegar and salt in large bowl; stir until salt is completely dissolved. Add shallots, chives, lemon juice and pepper; mix well. Slowly whisk in oil until well blended.

2. Add tomatoes to marinade; toss well. Cover; let stand at room temperature 30 minutes or up to 2 hours before serving.

3. Divide salad equally among 8 plates. Garnish with sunflower sprouts.   *Makes 8 servings*

Nutrients per serving: 1¼ cups salad

Calories	72	Carbohydrate	9 g
Calories from Fat	45 %	Cholesterol	0 mg
Fat	4 g	Sodium	163 mg
Saturated Fat	<1 g	Fiber	2 g
Protein	2 g		

Dietary Exchanges: 1½ Vegetable, 1 Fat

Italian Crouton Salad

6 ounces French or Italian bread
¼ cup plain fat-free yogurt
¼ cup red wine vinegar
4 teaspoons olive oil
1 tablespoon water
3 cloves garlic, minced
6 medium plum tomatoes, sliced (about 3¾ to 4 cups)
½ medium red onion, thinly sliced
3 tablespoons sliced fresh basil
2 tablespoons finely chopped fresh parsley
12 leaves red leaf lettuce *or* 4 cups prepared Italian salad mix
2 tablespoons grated Parmesan cheese

1. Preheat broiler. Cut bread into ¾-inch cubes; place in single layer on baking sheet. Broil 4 inches from heat 3 minutes or until bread is golden, stirring every 30 seconds to 1 minute. Place croutons in large bowl.

2. Whisk together yogurt, vinegar, oil, water and garlic in small bowl until blended; set aside. Add tomatoes, onion, basil and parsley to croutons; stir to combine. Pour yogurt mixture over crouton mixture; toss to coat. Cover; refrigerate 30 minutes or up to 1 day. (Croutons will be softer the following day.)

3. Place lettuce on 6 plates. Evenly divide crouton mixture over lettuce. Sprinkle with cheese.

Makes 6 servings

Side Salads

<u>Nutrients per serving:</u> ⅙ of total recipe

Calories	160	Carbohydrate	25 g
Calories from Fat	28 %	Cholesterol	2 mg
Fat	5 g	Sodium	234 mg
Saturated Fat	1 g	Fiber	2 g
Protein	6 g		

Dietary Exchanges: 1½ Vegetable, 1 Starch, 1 Fat

Raspberry Mango Salad

2 cups baby spinach or arugula
1 cup torn Bibb or Boston lettuce
1 cup diced peeled mango (about 1)
¾ cup fresh raspberries
½ cup stemmed watercress
¼ cup (1½ ounces) crumbled blue cheese
1 tablespoon water
1 tablespoon olive oil
1 tablespoon raspberry or red wine vinegar
⅛ teaspoon salt
⅛ teaspoon black pepper

1. Combine spinach, lettuce, mango, raspberries, watercress and cheese in medium bowl.

2. Place water, oil, vinegar, salt and pepper in small jar with tight-fitting lid; shake well. Pour over salad; toss to coat. Serve immediately. *Makes 4 servings*

Nutrients per serving: ¼ of total recipe

Calories	98	Carbohydrate	12 g
Calories from Fat	74 %	Cholesterol	8 mg
Fat	8 g	Sodium	227 mg
Saturated Fat	3 g	Fiber	2 g
Protein	3 g		

Dietary Exchanges: 2 Vegetable, 2 Fat

Greens and Broccoli Salad with Peppy Vinaigrette

    4 sun-dried tomato halves (not packed in oil)
    3 cups torn leaf lettuce
 1½ cups broccoli florets
    1 cup sliced mushrooms
    ⅓ cup sliced radishes
    2 tablespoons water
    1 tablespoon balsamic vinegar
    1 teaspoon vegetable oil
    ¼ teaspoon chicken bouillon granules
    ¼ teaspoon dried chervil or dried parsley
    ¼ teaspoon dry mustard
    ⅛ teaspoon ground red pepper

1. Pour boiling water over tomatoes in small bowl to cover. Let stand 5 minutes; drain.

2. Chop tomatoes. Combine tomatoes, lettuce, broccoli, mushrooms and radishes in large salad bowl.

3. Combine 2 tablespoons water, vinegar, oil, bouillon granules, chervil, mustard and red pepper in jar with tight-fitting lid; shake well. Add to salad; toss gently.

Makes 4 servings

Nutrients per serving: ¼ of total recipe

Calories	54	Carbohydrate	9 g
Calories from Fat	23 %	Cholesterol	0 mg
Fat	2 g	Sodium	79 mg
Saturated Fat	<1 g	Fiber	2 g
Protein	3 g		

Dietary Exchanges: 2 Vegetable

Lime-Ginger Cole Slaw

2 cups shredded green cabbage
1 cup shredded red cabbage
1½ cups matchstick-size carrots
¼ cup finely chopped green onions
3 tablespoons lime juice
2 tablespoons sugar substitute or sugar
2 tablespoons chopped fresh cilantro
2 teaspoons vegetable or canola oil
1½ teaspoons grated fresh ginger
⅛ teaspoon salt
⅛ teaspoon red pepper flakes (optional)

Combine cabbage, carrots, green onions, lime juice, sugar substitute, cilantro, oil, ginger, salt and red pepper flakes, if desired, in large bowl. Toss well. Let stand 10 minutes before serving.   *Makes 4 servings*

Nutrients per serving: ¼ of total recipe

Calories	58	**Carbohydrate**	10 g
Calories from Fat	7 %	**Cholesterol**	0 mg
Fat	2 g	**Sodium**	106 mg
Saturated Fat	1 g	**Fiber**	2 g
Protein	2 g		

Dietary Exchanges: 2 Vegetable

Fresh Cranberry-Pineapple Salad

1 medium orange
1 cup fresh or thawed frozen cranberries
$\frac{2}{3}$ cup water
1 package (4-serving size) sugar-free raspberry-flavored gelatin
1 cup ice cubes
$\frac{1}{2}$ (8-ounce) can crushed pineapple in juice, drained

1. Grate orange peel into small bowl; set aside. Coarsely chop cranberries in blender or food processor; set aside.

2. Squeeze juice from orange into small saucepan. Stir in water. Bring to a boil over high heat; remove from heat. Stir in gelatin until completely dissolved. Add ice cubes; stir until gelatin is slightly thickened. Remove any unmelted ice.

3. Stir in cranberries, pineapple and reserved orange peel. Pour mixture into 4 (6-ounce) glass dishes or 9-inch glass pie plate. Cover; refrigerate until firm.

Makes 4 servings

Nutrients per serving: ½ cup salad

Calories	59	**Carbohydrate**	13 g
Calories from Fat	2 %	**Cholesterol**	0 mg
Fat	<1 g	**Sodium**	56 mg
Saturated Fat	<1 g	**Fiber**	2 g
Protein	2 g		

Dietary Exchanges: 1 Fruit

Greens and Pears with Maple-Mustard Dressing

2 tablespoons plus 2 teaspoons chopped walnuts
¼ cup maple syrup
1 tablespoon Dijon mustard
1 tablespoon olive oil
1 tablespoon balsamic or cider vinegar
⅛ teaspoon black pepper
4 cups torn mixed salad greens
1 medium red pear, cored and thinly sliced
¼ cup sliced green onions
3 tablespoons dried tart cherries

1. Place walnuts in small skillet over medium heat. Cook and stir 5 minutes or until fragrant and lightly toasted. Transfer to plate to cool.

2. Whisk together syrup, mustard, oil, vinegar and pepper in small bowl.

3. Combine greens, pear slices, green onions, cherries and walnuts in large salad bowl. Drizzle with syrup mixture; toss gently. *Makes 4 servings*

Nutrients per serving: ¼ of total recipe

Calories	170	Carbohydrate	29 g
Calories from Fat	27 %	Cholesterol	0 mg
Fat	5 g	Sodium	184 mg
Saturated Fat	1 g	Fiber	3 g
Protein	1 g		

Dietary Exchanges: 1 Vegetable, 1½ Fruit, 1 Fat

Main-Course Salads

╰─⟲─⟳─╯

Mediterranean Chicken Salad

2 cups spring salad greens
½ cup diced or shredded cooked boneless
skinless chicken breast
1 plum tomato, sliced
¼ cup fat-free croutons
2 tablespoons chopped fresh basil
2 tablespoons reduced-fat reduced-sodium
Italian salad dressing
Black pepper (optional)

1. Combine greens, chicken, tomato, croutons, basil and dressing in large bowl; toss well.

2. Transfer mixture to plate. Season with pepper, if desired.   *Makes 1 serving*

<u>**Nutrients per serving**</u>: 1 salad

Calories	187	**Carbohydrate**	14 g
Calories from Fat	17 %	**Cholesterol**	56 mg
Fat	3 g	**Sodium**	587 mg
Saturated Fat	<1 g	**Fiber**	3 g
Protein	23 g		

Dietary Exchanges: 1 Vegetable, ½ Starch, 2 Meat

Finger-Lickin' Chicken Salad

½ **cup diced roasted skinless chicken**
½ **stalk celery, cut into 1-inch pieces**
¼ **cup drained mandarin orange segments**
¼ **cup red seedless grapes**
2 **tablespoons lemon sugar-free fat-free yogurt**
1 **tablespoon reduced-fat mayonnaise**
¼ **teaspoon reduced-sodium soy sauce**
⅛ **teaspoon pumpkin pie spice or cinnamon**

1. Combine chicken, celery, oranges and grapes in small bowl. Combine yogurt, mayonnaise, soy sauce and pumpkin pie spice in separate small bowl.

2. Drizzle yogurt mixture over chicken mixture; toss to coat.   *Makes 1 serving*

Note: For a picnic or packed lunch, place chicken mixture and dipping sauce in separate covered plastic containers. Pack in insulated bag with ice pack.

Nutrients per serving: 1 salad

Calories	207	Carbohydrate	15 g
Calories from Fat	25 %	Cholesterol	64 mg
Fat	6 g	Sodium	212 mg
Saturated Fat	1 g	Fiber	1 g
Protein	24 g		

Dietary Exchanges: 1 Fruit, 3 Lean Meat

Turkey Club Salad

8 large romaine lettuce leaves
**8 thin slices reduced-fat reduced-sodium
    deli-style turkey breast (about 4 ounces total)**
2 medium tomatoes, cut into 8 slices each
**2 tablespoons soy-based imitation bacon bits or
    real bacon bits**
¼ cup fat-free ranch salad dressing
    Black pepper (optional)

Layer lettuce, turkey, tomato and bacon bits on 2 plates.
Drizzle with dressing. Season with pepper, if desired.

Makes 2 servings

Nutrients per serving: ½ of total recipe

Calories	170	Carbohydrate	18 g
Calories from Fat	15 %	Cholesterol	23 mg
Fat	3 g	Sodium	521 mg
Saturated Fat	<1 g	Fiber	4 g
Protein	17 g		

Dietary Exchanges: 3 Vegetable, 2 Meat

Chicken and Apple Spring Green Salad with Poppy Seed Dressing

1 package (5 ounces) spring salad greens
12 ounces cooked chicken strips
1 large Golden Delicious apple, unpeeled and
     thinly sliced
⅓ cup thinly sliced red onion
1 ounce crumbled goat cheese (optional)
¼ cup cider vinegar
2 tablespoons sugar substitute
2 tablespoons canola oil
½ teaspoon poppy seeds
¼ teaspoon salt
⅛ teaspoon red pepper flakes

1. Arrange equal amounts greens, chicken, apple and onion on 4 plates. Sprinkle with cheese, if desired.

2. Combine vinegar, sugar substitute, oil, poppy seeds, salt and pepper flakes in small jar with tight-fitting lid; shake well. Drizzle dressing over salads.

Makes 4 servings

Nutrients per serving: ¼ of total recipe

Calories	224	Carbohydrate	8 g
Calories from Fat	40 %	Cholesterol	43 mg
Fat	10 g	Sodium	206 mg
Saturated Fat	1 g	Fiber	2 g
Protein	26 g		

Dietary Exchanges: 1 Vegetable, 1 Fruit, 3 Meat, 2 Fat

Gazpacho Shrimp Salad

½ cup chunky salsa
1 tablespoon balsamic vinegar
1 tablespoon extra-virgin olive oil
1 clove garlic, minced
8 cups torn mixed salad greens or romaine
lettuce
1 large tomato, chopped
1 small ripe avocado, diced
½ cup thinly sliced unpeeled cucumber
½ pound large cooked shrimp, peeled and
deveined
½ cup coarsely chopped fresh cilantro

1. Combine salsa, vinegar, oil and garlic in small bowl; blend well.

2. Combine greens, tomato, avocado and cucumber in large bowl. Divide salad evenly among 4 plates; top with shrimp. Drizzle dressing over salads. Sprinkle with cilantro. *Makes 4 servings*

Nutrients per serving: ¼ of total recipe

Calories	190	Carbohydrate	10 g
Calories from Fat	50 %	Cholesterol	111 mg
Fat	11 g	Sodium	312 mg
Saturated Fat	2 g	Fiber	5 g
Protein	14 g		

Dietary Exchanges: 2 Vegetable, 2 Meat, 1 Fat

Healthy Chopped Salad

10 ounces cooked skinless turkey breast, chopped
1 small head bok choy, chopped
2 cups baby spinach, chopped
1 tomato, chopped
1 cup baby carrots, chopped
1 package (8 ounces) sugar snap peas, chopped
2 romaine lettuce hearts, chopped
Juice of 1 lemon (about ¼ cup)
Juice of 1 lime (about ¼ cup)
1 tablespoon creamy peanut butter
2 teaspoons sugar substitute
2 teaspoons sesame seeds
1 teaspoon minced garlic
½ teaspoon black pepper (optional)

1. Place turkey, bok choy, spinach, tomato, carrots, snap peas and romaine in large bowl; set aside.

2. Combine lemon juice, lime juice, peanut butter, sugar substitute, sesame seeds, garlic and pepper, if desired, in jar with tight-fitting lid; shake well.

3. Pour dressing over salad; toss well.

Makes 8 servings

<u>**Nutrients per serving:**</u> ⅛ of total recipe

Calories	96	Carbohydrate	7 g
Calories from Fat	16%	Cholesterol	29 mg
Fat	2 g	Sodium	174 mg
Saturated Fat	<1 g	Fiber	2 g
Protein	13 g		

Dietary Exchanges: 2 Vegetable, 1 Meat

Zesty Taco Salad

2 tablespoons canola oil
1 tablespoon red wine vinegar
1 clove garlic, minced
¾ pound 93% lean ground turkey
1¾ teaspoons chili powder
¼ teaspoon ground cumin
3 cups torn lettuce leaves
1 can (about 14 ounces) Mexican-style diced
   tomatoes, drained
1 cup canned chickpeas or pinto beans, rinsed
   and drained
⅔ cup chopped peeled cucumber
⅓ cup frozen corn, thawed
¼ cup chopped red onion
1 to 2 jalapeño peppers,* seeded and finely
   chopped (optional)
12 fat-free tortilla chips

*Jalapeño peppers can sting and irritate the skin, so
wear rubber gloves when handling peppers and do not
touch your eyes.*

1. Combine oil, vinegar and garlic in small bowl.

2. Combine turkey, chili powder and cumin in large
nonstick skillet. Cook over medium heat 5 minutes or
until turkey is cooked through, stirring to break up meat.

3. Combine turkey, lettuce, tomatoes, chickpeas,
cucumber, corn, onion and jalapeño, if desired, in large
bowl. Add dressing; toss to coat. Serve on tortilla chips.

Makes 4 servings

Main-Course Salads

Nutrients per serving: 1½ cups salad with 3 tortilla chips

Calories	285	Carbohydrate	28 g
Calories from Fat	33 %	Cholesterol	33 mg
Fat	11 g	Sodium	484 mg
Saturated Fat	1 g	Fiber	5 g
Protein	21 g		

Dietary Exchanges: 1 Vegetable, 1½ Starch, 2 Meat, 1 Fat

Three-Pepper Tuna Salad

2 cups thinly sliced zucchini
½ cup red bell pepper strips
½ cup green bell pepper strips
½ cup yellow bell pepper strips
1 cup cherry tomatoes, halved
1 can (6 ounces) solid albacore tuna packed in water, drained and flaked
¼ cup chopped green onions
¼ cup chopped fresh basil
2 tablespoons red wine vinegar
1 tablespoon olive oil
½ teaspoon minced garlic
½ teaspoon chopped fresh marjoram *or*
¼ teaspoon dried marjoram
⅛ teaspoon black pepper

1. Bring ¾ cup water to a boil over high heat in medium saucepan. Add zucchini and bell peppers. Reduce heat. Cover and simmer 10 minutes or until crisp-tender; drain well. Transfer to serving bowl. Add tomatoes, tuna, green onions and basil.

2. Combine vinegar, oil, garlic, marjoram and black pepper in jar with tight-fitting lid; shake well. Pour dressing over salad; mix well.   *Makes 4 servings*

Nutrients per serving: ¼ of total recipe

Calories	134	Carbohydrate	11 g
Calories from Fat	34 %	Cholesterol	18 mg
Fat	5 g	Sodium	175 mg
Saturated Fat	1 g	Fiber	3 g
Protein	14 g		

Dietary Exchanges: 2 Vegetable, 1½ Meat

Chicken and Pasta Salad with Kalamata Olives

    4 ounces uncooked multigrain rotini
    2 cups diced cooked chicken
    ½ cup chopped roasted red bell peppers
    12 pitted kalamata or black olives, halved
    1 tablespoon dried basil
    4½ teaspoons olive oil
    1 tablespoon cider vinegar
    1 to 2 cloves garlic, minced
    ¼ teaspoon salt (optional)

1. Cook rotini according to package directions, omitting salt and fat. Drain well; cool.

2. Combine chicken, peppers, olives, basil, oil, vinegar, garlic and salt, if desired, in medium bowl.

3. Add cooled pasta to chicken mixture; toss gently. Divide equally among 4 plates.   *Makes 4 servings*

<u>**Nutrients per serving**</u>: ¼ of total recipe

Calories	276	Carbohydrate	25 g
Calories from Fat	29 %	Cholesterol	54 mg
Fat	9 g	Sodium	341 mg
Saturated Fat	2 g	Fiber	3 g
Protein	25 g		

Dietary Exchanges: 1½ Starch, 3 Meat

Salmon and Green Bean Salad with Pasta

8 ounces small whole wheat or regular pasta shells
¾ cup fresh green beans, cut into 2-inch pieces
⅔ cup finely chopped carrots
1 can (6 ounces) red salmon, drained and flaked
½ cup fat-free cottage cheese
3 tablespoons plain fat-free yogurt
1½ tablespoons lemon juice
1 tablespoon chopped fresh dill *or* 1 teaspoon dried dill weed
2 teaspoons grated onion
1 teaspoon Dijon mustard

1. Cook pasta according to package directions, including ¼ teaspoon salt; add green beans during last 3 minutes of cooking. Drain; rinse under cold running water until pasta and green beans are cool. Drain well.

2. Combine pasta, green beans, carrots and salmon in medium bowl.

3. Place cottage cheese, yogurt, lemon juice, dill, onion and mustard in food processor or blender; process until smooth. Pour over pasta mixture; toss to coat.

Makes 6 servings

Nutrients per serving: ⅙ of total recipe

Calories	210	Carbohydrate	29 g
Calories from Fat	15 %	Cholesterol	15 mg
Fat	3 g	Sodium	223 mg
Saturated Fat	1 g	Fiber	2 g
Protein	16 g		

Dietary Exchanges: ½ Vegetable, 1½ Starch, 1½ Meat

Super Soups

Winter Squash Soup

1 tablespoon low-fat vegetable oil spread
1 tablespoon minced onion or shallot
2 cloves garlic, minced
3 fresh thyme sprigs *or* ¼ teaspoon dried thyme
   Pinch dried rosemary
2 packages (10 ounces each) frozen butternut squash, thawed
1 cup fat-free reduced-sodium chicken broth
3 tablespoons fat-free (skim) milk
   Fat-free sour cream (optional)

1. Melt spread in medium saucepan over medium heat. Add onion, garlic, thyme and rosemary. Cook and stir 2 to 3 minutes or until onion is tender. Add squash and broth; bring to a boil. Add milk; stir until blended.

2. Remove thyme sprigs from soup. Working in batches, place mixture in blender or food processor; process until smooth. (Add additional broth or water to make soup thinner, if desired.) Top each serving with dollop of sour cream, if desired.   *Makes 4 servings*

Nutrients per serving: 1 cup soup

Calories	116	**Carbohydrate**	22 g
Calories from Fat	16 %	**Cholesterol**	<1 mg
Fat	2 g	**Sodium**	135 mg
Saturated Fat	<1 g	**Fiber**	2 g
Protein	5 g		

Dietary Exchanges: 4 Vegetable, ½ Fat

Country Sausage and Bean Soup

2 cans (about 14 ounces each) reduced-sodium chicken broth
1½ cups hot water
1 cup dried black beans, rinsed and sorted
1 cup chopped yellow onion
2 bay leaves
1 teaspoon sugar substitute
⅛ teaspoon ground red pepper
Nonstick cooking spray
6 ounces reduced-fat bulk pork sausage
1 cup chopped tomato
1 tablespoon chili powder
1 tablespoon Worcestershire sauce
2 teaspoons olive oil
1½ teaspoons ground cumin
½ teaspoon salt
¼ cup chopped fresh cilantro

SLOW COOKER DIRECTIONS

1. Combine broth, water, beans, onion, bay leaves, sugar substitute and red pepper in slow cooker. Cover; cook on LOW 8 hours or on HIGH 4 hours.

2. Coat large nonstick skillet with cooking spray. Brown sausage over medium heat, stirring to break up meat; drain fat.

3. Add sausage, tomato, chili powder, Worcestershire sauce, oil, cumin and salt to slow cooker. Cover; cook on HIGH 15 minutes. Remove and discard bay leaves. Ladle soup into bowls; sprinkle each serving with cilantro.

Makes 9 servings

Super Soups

Nutrients per serving: ¾ cup soup

Calories	159	**Carbohydrate**	17 g
Calories from Fat	31 %	**Cholesterol**	23 mg
Fat	6 g	**Sodium**	360 mg
Saturated Fat	1 g	**Fiber**	4 g
Protein	11 g		

Dietary Exchanges: 1 Starch, 1 Meat, 1 Fat

Deep Bayou Chowder

Nonstick cooking spray
1½ cups chopped onions
1 large green bell pepper, chopped
1 large carrot, chopped
8 ounces red potatoes, diced
1 cup frozen corn
1 cup water
½ teaspoon dried thyme
2 cups fat-free (skim) milk
2 tablespoons chopped parsley
1½ teaspoons seafood seasoning
¾ teaspoon salt (optional)

1. Spray Dutch oven with cooking spray; heat over medium-high heat. Add onions, pepper and carrot; spray with cooking spray. Cook and stir 4 minutes or until onions are translucent.

2. Add potatoes, corn, water and thyme; bring to a boil over high heat. Reduce heat; cover and simmer 15 minutes or until potatoes are tender. Stir in milk, parsley, seasoning and salt, if desired. Cook 5 minutes more. *Makes 6 servings*

Nutrients per serving: 1 cup soup

Calories	102	Carbohydrate	21 g
Calories from Fat	4%	Cholesterol	2 mg
Fat	1 g	Sodium	121 mg
Saturated Fat	1 g	Fiber	3 g
Protein	5 g		

Dietary Exchanges: 1½ Starch

Beef and Veggie Soup

3 teaspoons olive oil, divided
12 ounces trimmed boneless beef top sirloin, cut into bite-size pieces
2 medium carrots, quartered lengthwise and cut into 2-inch pieces
1 medium green bell pepper, coarsely chopped
6 ounces green beans, cut into 2-inch pieces
1 can (about 14 ounces) Italian-style stewed tomatoes
1 cup beef broth
8 ounces new potatoes, cut into bite-size pieces
3 teaspoons instant coffee granules, divided
¾ teaspoon salt (optional)
¼ teaspoon black pepper

1. Heat 2 teaspoons oil in Dutch oven over medium-high heat. Brown beef 1 to 2 minutes; remove to plate.

2. Add remaining 1 teaspoon oil, carrots, bell pepper and green beans to Dutch oven. Cook and stir 4 minutes or until edges begin to brown. Add tomatoes, broth, potatoes and 1 teaspoon coffee granules; bring to a boil. Reduce heat. Add beef; cover and simmer 20 minutes or until potatoes are tender.

3. Stir in remaining 2 teaspoons coffee granules, salt, if desired, and black pepper. *Makes 4 servings*

Super Soups

Nutrients per serving: 1½ cups soup

Calories	265	Carbohydrate	28 g
Calories from Fat	23 %	Cholesterol	31 mg
Fat	7 g	Sodium	589 mg
Saturated Fat	2 g	Fiber	5 g
Protein	23 g		

Dietary Exchanges: 2 Starch, 2 Meat

Chilled Roasted Red Pepper Soup

3 large red bell peppers
3 cups vegetable broth
1 cup water
1 cup diced onion
1 tablespoon minced garlic
1 bay leaf
½ teaspoon celery seeds
½ teaspoon black pepper
2 dashes hot sauce
Plain fat-free yogurt (optional)

1. Preheat oven to 400°F. Place peppers on baking sheet; roast about 30 minutes, turning every 10 minutes, until charred. Transfer peppers to brown paper bag. Close bag; set aside 10 minutes. Remove skin from peppers. Cut peppers into quarters. Remove and discard seeds and ribs.

2. Place roasted peppers, broth, water, onion, garlic, bay leaf, celery seeds, black pepper and hot sauce in large saucepan. Cover; cook over medium heat 45 minutes. Remove and discard bay leaf. Cool soup 15 minutes. Working in batches, place mixture in blender or food processor; process until smooth.

3. Chill soup in refrigerator 3 hours or overnight before serving. Serve with dollop of yogurt, if desired.

Makes 6 servings

Super Soups

Nutrients per serving: ¾ cup soup

Calories	45	Carbohydrate	9 g
Calories from Fat	9 %	Cholesterol	0 mg
Fat	<1 g	Sodium	233 mg
Saturated Fat	<1 g	Fiber	2 g
Protein	1 g		

Dietary Exchanges: 2 Vegetable

Hearty Lentil and Root Vegetable Soup

   2 cans (about 14 ounces each) chicken broth
1½ cups diced turnip
   1 cup dried red or brown lentils, rinsed and sorted
   1 medium onion, cut into ½-inch wedges
   2 medium carrots, cut into 1-inch pieces
   1 medium red bell pepper, cut into 1-inch pieces
 ½ teaspoon dried oregano
 ⅛ teaspoon red pepper flakes
   1 tablespoon olive oil
 ½ teaspoon salt
   4 slices bacon, crisp-cooked and crumbled
 ½ cup finely chopped green onions

SLOW COOKER DIRECTIONS

1. Combine broth, turnip, lentils, onion, carrots, bell pepper, oregano and pepper flakes in 4-quart slow cooker. Cover; cook on LOW 6 hours or on HIGH 3 hours or until lentils are tender.

2. Stir in olive oil and salt. Ladle into bowls; sprinkle each serving with bacon and green onions.

Makes 8 servings

<u>Nutrients per serving:</u> about ¾ cup soup

Calories	164	Carbohydrate	21 g
Calories from Fat	22%	Cholesterol	14 mg
Fat	4 g	Sodium	355 mg
Saturated Fat	<1 g	Fiber	9 g
Protein	12 g		

Dietary Exchanges: 1 Vegetable, 1 Starch, 1 Meat

French Peasant Soup

1 slice lean bacon, chopped
½ cup diced carrots
½ cup diced celery
¼ cup minced onion
1 clove garlic, minced
2 tablespoons white wine or water
1½ cups fat-free reduced-sodium vegetable broth
1 sprig fresh thyme *or* 1 teaspoon dried thyme
1 bay leaf
1 sprig fresh parsley *or* 1 teaspoon dried parsley
½ cup green beans, cut into ½-inch pieces
2 tablespoons small pasta or elbow macaroni
½ cup no-salt-added canned cannellini beans,
    rinsed and drained
½ cup diced zucchini
¼ cup chopped leek or onion
2 teaspoons prepared pesto sauce
2 teaspoons grated Parmesan cheese

1. Cook bacon in medium saucepan over medium heat 3 minutes or until partially cooked; drain fat. Add carrots, celery, onion and garlic; cook 5 minutes or until carrots are crisp-tender. Stir in wine; simmer until most of wine has evaporated. Add broth, thyme, bay leaf and parsley; simmer 10 minutes.

2. Add green beans; simmer 5 minutes. Add pasta; cook 5 to 7 minutes or until almost tender. Add cannellini beans, zucchini and leek; cook 3 to 5 minutes or until vegetables are tender.

3. Remove and discard bay leaf. Ladle soup into 2 bowls. Stir 1 teaspoon pesto into each bowl; sprinkle each with 1 teaspoon cheese. *Makes 2 servings*

Super Soups

Nutrients per serving: ½ of total recipe

Calories	192	Carbohydrate	30 g
Calories from Fat	16 %	Cholesterol	6 mg
Fat	3 g	Sodium	499 mg
Saturated Fat	1 g	Fiber	7 g
Protein	9 g		

Dietary Exchanges: 1½ Starch, 1 Fat

Main-Dish Chicken Soup

6 cups fat-free reduced-sodium chicken broth
1 cup grated carrots
½ cup diced red bell pepper
½ cup frozen green peas
½ cup sliced green onions
1 seedless cucumber
12 chicken tenders (about 1 pound), halved
½ teaspoon white pepper

1. Bring broth to a boil in Dutch oven. Add carrots, bell pepper, peas and green onions. Return to a boil. Reduce heat; simmer 3 minutes.

2. Meanwhile, cut ends off cucumber and discard. Using vegetable peeler, start at top and make long, noodle-like strips of cucumber. Cut any remaining cucumber pieces into thin slices. Add cucumber to Dutch oven; cook 2 minutes over low heat.

3. Add chicken tenders and white pepper; simmer 5 minutes or until chicken is cooked through.

Makes 6 servings

Nutrients per serving: 1¾ cups soup

Calories	158	Carbohydrate	7 g
Calories from Fat	15 %	Cholesterol	68 mg
Fat	3 g	Sodium	304 mg
Saturated Fat	<1 g	Fiber	2 g
Protein	26 g		

Dietary Exchanges: 1½ Vegetable, 2½ Meat

Cuban-Style Black Bean Soup

2 teaspoons olive oil
1 small onion, chopped
1 cup thinly sliced carrots
2 jalapeño peppers,* seeded and minced
2 cloves garlic, minced
1 can (about 15 ounces) no-salt-added black
    beans, undrained
1 can (about 14 ounces) vegetable or chicken
    broth
¼ cup reduced-fat sour cream
¼ cup chopped fresh cilantro
4 lime wedges (optional)

Jalapeño peppers can sting and irritate the skin, so wear rubber gloves when handling peppers and do not touch your eyes.

1. Heat oil in large saucepan over medium heat. Add onion, carrots, jalapeños and garlic; cook and stir 5 minutes.

2. Add beans and broth; bring to a boil. Cover; reduce heat to low. Simmer 15 to 20 minutes or until vegetables are very tender.

3. Ladle soup into bowls; top each serving with sour cream and cilantro. Serve with lime wedges, if desired.

Makes 4 servings

Note: Soup will be chunky. If desired, process soup in a food processor or blender until smooth.

Super Soups

Nutrients per serving: 1 cup soup

Calories	163	Carbohydrate	25 g
Calories from Fat	21 %	Cholesterol	5 mg
Fat	4 g	Sodium	245 mg
Saturated Fat	1 g	Fiber	7 g
Protein	8 g		

Dietary Exchanges: 1½ Starch, 1 Meat

Creamy Cauliflower Bisque

1 pound frozen cauliflower florets
1 pound baking potatoes, peeled and cut into
**   1-inch cubes**
2 cans (about 14 ounces each) fat-free
**   reduced-sodium chicken broth**
1 cup chopped yellow onion
½ teaspoon dried thyme
¼ teaspoon garlic powder
⅛ teaspoon ground red pepper
1 cup fat-free evaporated milk
2 tablespoons butter
½ teaspoon salt
¼ teaspoon black pepper
1 cup (4 ounces) shredded reduced-fat sharp
**   Cheddar cheese**
¼ cup finely chopped fresh parsley
¼ cup finely chopped green onions

SLOW COOKER DIRECTIONS

1. Combine cauliflower, potatoes, broth, onion, thyme, garlic powder and red pepper in slow cooker. Cover; cook on LOW 8 hours or on HIGH 4 hours.

2. Working in batches, place soup in blender or food processor; process until smooth. Return to slow cooker. Add milk, butter, salt and black pepper. Cook, uncovered, on HIGH 30 minutes or until heated through.

3. Ladle into bowls; top each serving with cheese, parsley and green onions.   *Makes 9 servings*

Super Soups

Nutrients per serving: about ¾ cup soup

Calories	158	Carbohydrate	19 g
Calories from Fat	27 %	Cholesterol	19 mg
Fat	5 g	Sodium	410 mg
Saturated Fat	2 g	Fiber	3 g
Protein	10 g		

Dietary Exchanges: 1 Starch, 1 Meat, ½ Fat

Tomato-Herb Soup

1 can (about 14 ounces) no-salt-added diced tomatoes
1 can (about 14 ounces) reduced-sodium chicken broth
½ cup water
1 bag (8 ounces) frozen bell pepper stir-fry mixture
1 cup frozen green beans
1 tablespoon ketchup
1 to 2 teaspoons dried oregano
1 teaspoon dried basil
⅛ teaspoon red pepper flakes (optional)
1 tablespoon olive oil
½ teaspoon salt (optional)

1. Combine tomatoes, broth, water, bell peppers, green beans, ketchup, oregano, basil and pepper flakes, if desired, in large saucepan. Bring to a boil over high heat. Reduce heat. Cover; simmer 20 minutes or until beans are tender and mixture has thickened slightly.

2. Remove from heat. Stir in oil and salt, if desired. Let stand 5 minutes before serving. *Makes 4 servings*

Variation: Substitute chopped fresh bell peppers for the frozen stir-fry mix.

<u>**Nutrients per serving:**</u> 1 cup soup

Calories	94	**Carbohydrate**	14 g
Calories from Fat	28 %	**Cholesterol**	0 mg
Fat	3 g	**Sodium**	327 mg
Saturated Fat	<1 g	**Fiber**	4 g
Protein	3 g		

Dietary Exchanges: 1 Starch, ½ Fat